S0-AIH-237

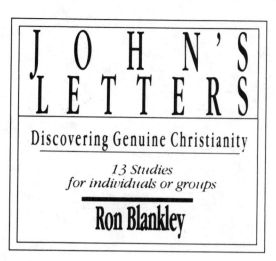

JOHN'S LETTERS

Discovering Genuine Christianity

13 Studies for individuals or groups

Ron Blankley

With Notes for Leaders

INTERVARSITY PRESS
DOWNERS GROVE, ILLINOIS 60515

© 1990 by Ron Blankley

All rights reserved. No part of this book may be reproduced in any form without written permission from InterVarsity Press, P.O. Box 1400, Downers Grove, IL 60515.

InterVarsity Press is the book-publishing division of InterVarsity Christian Fellowship, a student movement active on campus at hundreds of universities, colleges and schools of nursing. For information about local and regional activities, write Public Relations Dept., InterVarsity Christian Fellowship, 6400 Schroeder Rd., P.O. Box 7895, Madison, WI 53707-7895.

All Scripture quotations, unless otherwise indicated, are taken from the Holy Bible, New International Version. Copyright © 1973, 1978, International Bible Society. Used by permission of Zondervan Bible Publishers.

Cover photograph: Robert McKendrick

ISBN 0-8308-1020-X

Printed in the United States of America

18	17	16	15	14	13	12	11	10	9	8	7	6		
99	98	97	96	95	94									

Contents

Getting the Most
from LifeGuide Bible Studies

Many of us long to fill our minds and our lives with Scripture. We desire to be transformed by its message. LifeGuide Bible Studies are designed to be an exciting and challenging way to do just that. They help us to be guided by God's Word in every area of life.

How They Work

LifeGuides have a number of distinctive features. Perhaps the most important is that they are *inductive* rather than *deductive*. In other words, they lead us to *discover* what the Bible says rather than simply *telling* us what it says.

They are also thought provoking. They help us to think about the meaning of the passage so that we can truly understand what the author is saying. The questions require more than one-word answers.

The studies are personal. Questions expose us to the promises, assurances, exhortations and challenges of God's Word. They are designed to allow the Scriptures to renew our minds so that we can be transformed by the Spirit of God. This is the ultimate goal of all Bible study.

The studies are versatile. They are designed for student, neighborhood and church groups. They are also effective for individual study.

How They're Put Together

LifeGuides also have a distinctive format. Each study need take no more than forty-five minutes in a group setting or thirty minutes in personal study—unless you choose to take more time.

The studies can be used within a quarter system in a church and fit well in a semester or trimester system on a college campus. If a guide has more than thirteen studies, it is divided into two or occasionally three parts of approximately twelve studies each.

LifeGuides use a workbook format. Space is provided for writing answers to each question. This is ideal for personal study and allows group members to prepare in advance for the discussion.

The studies also contain leader's notes. They show how to lead a group discussion, provide additional background information on certain questions, give helpful tips on group dynamics and suggest ways to deal with problems which may arise during the discussion. With such helps, someone with little or no experience can lead an effective study.

Suggestions for Individual Study

1. As you begin each study, pray that God will help you to understand and apply the passage to your life.

2. Read and reread the assigned Bible passage to familiarize yourself with what the author is saying. In the case of book studies, you may want to read through the entire book prior to the first study. This will give you a helpful overview of its contents.

3. A good modern translation of the Bible, rather than the King James Version or a paraphrase, will give you the most help. The New International Version, the New American Standard Bible and the Revised Standard Version are all recommended. However, the questions in this guide are based on the New International Version.

4. Write your answers in the space provided in the study guide. This will help you to express your understanding of the passage clearly.

5. It might be good to have a Bible dictionary handy. Use it to look up any unfamiliar words, names or places.

Suggestions for Group Study

1. Come to the study prepared. Follow the suggestions for individual study mentioned above. You will find that careful preparation will greatly enrich your time spent in group discussion.

2. Be willing to participate in the discussion. The leader of your group will not be lecturing. Instead, he or she will be encouraging the members of the group to discuss what they have learned from the passage. The leader will be asking the questions that are found in this guide. Plan to share what God has taught you in your individual study.

3. Stick to the passage being studied. Your answers should be based on the verses which are the focus of the discussion and not on outside authorities such as commentaries or speakers. This guide deliberately avoids jumping

from book to book or passage to passage. Each study focuses on only one passage. Book studies are generally designed to lead you through the book in the order in which it was written. This will help you follow the author's argument.

4. Be sensitive to the other members of the group. Listen attentively when they share what they have learned. You may be surprised by their insights! Link what you say to the comments of others so the group stays on the topic. Also, be affirming whenever you can. This will encourage some of the more hesitant members of the group to participate.

5. Be careful not to dominate the discussion. We are sometimes so eager to share what we have learned that we leave too little opportunity for others to respond. By all means participate! But allow others to also.

6. Expect God to teach you through the passage being discussed and through the other members of the group. Pray that you will have an enjoyable and profitable time together.

7. If you are the discussion leader, you will find additional suggestions and helpful ideas for each study in the leader's notes. These are found at the back of the guide.

Introducing John's Letters

Today many people claim to be Christians. In fact, a 1986 Gallup Survey revealed that ninety-four per cent of adult Americans believe in God, and that seventy-six per cent believe that Jesus is either God or the Son of God. Furthermore, when the question was asked, "Would you describe yourself as a 'born again' Christian or not?" thirty-three percent said yes.

The problem, of course, is that actions speak louder than words. The same survey revealed that many of the mainline Protestant denominations have experienced sharp losses in membership since the mid-sixties. For example, only forty per cent told Gallup that they had attended church in the last week, and only ten per cent claimed to read the Bible on a daily basis.

This credibility problem is intensified when we move from the pew to the pulpit. A shocking number of Christian leaders have been found guilty of sexual sin or financial misconduct. Sadly, their moral failures have been brought to our national attention by the secular news media, anxious to expose such blatant hypocrisy. If such leaders are representative of the church in general, it seems that we are indeed experiencing a period of unprecedented moral decline.

How are we to respond to this kind of situation? How can we tell the difference between genuine Christians and those who merely profess to know Christ?

John's letters were written for that very purpose. John writes to expose the false claims of those whose conduct contradicts their claims. He also provides strong assurance to those whose lifestyle is consistent with their Christian faith.

Background to 1 John

First John was written between A.D. 85-95 by the Apostle John, the author of the Gospel of John and Revelation. Evidently the letter was circulated among a number of churches in Asia who were threatened by false teachers.

These false teachers embraced an early form of heresy known as Gnosticism. They taught that matter was entirely evil and spirit was entirely good. This teaching resulted in two fundamental errors:

A *"new" theology.* This centered in a denial of the incarnation. Since God could not be contaminated by a human body, these false teachers did not believe God became man in Jesus Christ. Some taught that he merely seemed to have a body, a view known as Docetism. Others claimed that the divine Christ descended on Jesus at his baptism but departed before the crucifixion, a view known as Cerinthianism. This latter view seems to be in the background of much of 1 John.

A *"new" morality.* These false teachers also claimed "to have reached such an advanced stage in spiritual experience that they were 'beyond good and evil.' They maintained that they had no sin, not in the sense that they had attained moral perfection but in the sense that what might be sin for people at a less mature stage of inner development was no longer sin for the completely 'spiritual' man. For him ethical distinctions had ceased to be relevant."[1]

What intensified this problem was that these false teachers had once been an active part of the fellowship which John's readers were continuing to enjoy (see 2:19). But because their "new" teaching was so contrary to the apostolic truths of the gospel, they had to part company with the faithful. As you can well imagine, those who remained in the true fellowship were unsettled and shaken by the defection of these new teachers and needed to be reassured. But in the process, the others also needed to be exposed for what they truly were—unbelieving heretics.

In order to accomplish both purposes, John provides a series of tests for distinguishing between genuine Christians and those who falsely claim to know Christ. In response to the "new" theology, he provides us with a doctrinal test: What does the person believe about Christ? In response to the "new" morality, he provides us with a moral test: How does the person respond to the commandments of Christ? Finally, he provides us with a social test: Does the person love other Christians?

In fact, John's entire first letter is structured around these three tests, each of which appears in three separate groups, or cycles, in the letter. After the prologue (1:1-4), there is the first cycle (1:5—2:27), followed by the second

(2:28—4:6) and third (4:7—5:12). Then in the conclusion (5:13-21), John again emphasizes his theme of Christian assurance.

In view of this purpose and structure, it is important to realize that the contrasts in John's letter are not between two types of Christians but between genuine Christians and those who merely claim to be Christians. For in the words of John Stott: "John's argument is double-edged. If he seeks to bring believers to the knowledge that they have eternal life, he is equally at pains to show that unbelievers have not. His purpose is to destroy the false assurance of the counterfeit as well as to confirm the right assurance of the genuine."[2]

Background to 2 John

Second John was also written by the Apostle John between A.D. 85-95. It was written to provide guidance about hospitality. During the first century, traveling evangelists relied on the hospitality of church members. Because inns were few and unsafe, believers would take such people into their homes and then give them provisions for their journey. Since Gnostic teachers also relied on hospitality, John warned his readers against taking such people into their homes lest they participate in spreading heresy.

Background to 3 John

Third John was also written to provide us with guidance about hospitality, but in a much more positive way. Whereas 2 John tells us what we are *not* to do, 3 John emphasizes what we *are* to do. For those genuine teachers who are totally dependent upon the Body of Christ for all of their needs, we are to open not only our hearts but also our homes. This instruction is primarily found in John's commendation of Gaius, who has done this very thing, and in his denunciation of Diotrephes, who has refused. These two men become living examples of good and evil, truth and error.

This LifeGuide contains thirteen studies in John's letters. The first ten cover 1 John, and the next two look at 2 & 3 John. The final study is a review of the three books. It is my hope that these studies will encourage and assure you that you "walk in the truth."

---

[1] F. F. Bruce, *The Epistles of John* (Grand Rapids, Mich.: Eerdmans, 1978), p. 26.
[2] John Stott, *The Epistles of John* (Grand Rapids, Mich.: Eerdmans, 1964), p. 52.

1
Fellowship & Forgiveness

1 John 1:1-10

Christians everywhere seem to be interested in fellowship. They gather in fellowship halls, attend fellowship dinners and participate in well-organized activities with fellow believers. But what really constitutes biblical fellowship? A covered dish supper? Coffee and doughnuts? Social events and activities? Perhaps more than any other passage of Scripture, these opening verses of 1 John establish the basis of true fellowship that is to be enjoyed and experienced by all Christians. More importantly, they enable us to understand how we can know we have fellowship with God.

1. What normally comes to your mind when you think of Christian fellowship?

2. Read 1 John 1:1-10. John begins this chapter by announcing an apostolic message. What is the content of that message (vv. 1-2)?

3. What are John's reasons for announcing his message (vv. 3-4)?

4. In light of this apostolic message, what is the foundation of our fellowship as Christians?

5. John provides a test by which we can know if we have fellowship with God (vv. 5-10). What kind of test is it?

6. The basis for this test is God's character (v. 5). What specifically do *light* and *darkness* symbolize (vv. 5-7; see Jn 3:19-21)?

7. The first part of John's test concerns the way we live or "walk" (vv. 6-7). What is the relationship between our conduct and our claim to have fellowship with God?

Is John describing Christians who are either in or out of fellowship with God, or Christians and those who really do not know God at all? Explain.

8. The second part of John's test concerns our attitude toward sin (vv. 8-10). What does our denial or confession of sin reveal about the reality of our relationship with God?

9. Based on your study of this passage, what does it mean to have fellowship with God and each other?

10. Does John's test strengthen or weaken your assurance of fellowship with God? Explain.

11. How can we enjoy a greater fellowship with those who know the Father and the Son?

2
Talking & Walking the Truth

1 John 2:1-11

From the very beginning of Jesus' ministry, he emphasized that it is not what we profess but what we *possess* that counts for eternity. In his first major message he declared, "By their fruit you will recognize them." He then went on to teach, "Not everyone who says to me, 'Lord, Lord,' will enter the kingdom of heaven, but only he who does the will of my Father who is in heaven" (Mt 7:20-21).

In the same way, John emphasizes that our claim to know Jesus must be backed by our conduct; our talk must be matched by our walk. Both are necessary if we are to be certain about the reality of our faith.

---

1. When people we know say one thing yet do another, which usually tells the truth about them? Why?

---

2. Read 1 John 2:1-11. Although John does not want us to sin, he knows that we sometimes do (vv. 1-2). How does the realization that Jesus speaks "in our defense" provide comfort and assurance when you sin?

3. How does the concept of *atoning sacrifice* (v. 2) help us understand the way Jesus "speaks" for us?

4. According to John, how can we tell whether we truly know Christ or merely claim to know him (vv. 3-6)?

What other conclusions does John make about those who obey or disobey Christ's commands?

5. Practically speaking, what does it mean to "walk as Jesus did" (v. 6)?

6. In verses 7-11, John focuses on one of the commands. How can this command be both old and new (vv. 7-8)?

7. Why would love for our brother rather than love for God serve as a test of being in the light (vv. 9-11)?

8. Compare John's statements about love and hate (vv. 9-11) with similar ones made later in the epistle (3:10, 14-15). How do these verses clarify the two types of people John is contrasting?

9. In view of the overall context of this passage, what does it mean to *live* in the light (v. 10)?

To live in Christ (v. 6)?

10. How does this passage encourage you to obey Christ and love other members of his Body?

3
Encouragement & Warning
1 John 2:12-17

Pilgrim's Progress is the classic tale of Christian's escape from the City of Destruction to the Heavenly City. It is true to experience because all of us can identify with his encounters along the way. In the Valley of Humiliation he enters into combat with Apollyon, his fiercest foe. At the Hill of Difficulty he meets Adam-the-First and his three daughters: the Lust-of-the-Flesh, the Lust-of-the-Eyes and the Pride-of-Life. In the town of Folly he narrowly escapes its greatest attraction, Vanity Fair.

These encounters are John Bunyan's well-known descriptions of the three-fold arena of all Christian conflict—the world, the flesh and the devil. They are the same three foes which appear here in 1 John. In a context of encouragement and warning, the apostle tells us something of the evil one, the enticement of the world and the sinful desires of the flesh.

1. How far did you progress as a Christian before you became aware of these three foes? Explain.

2. Read 1 John 2:12-17. Why would John want to give a word of encouragement at this point in his letter?

Why a word of warning?

_____

3. Who is represented by the three groups being addressed (vv. 12-14)?

How are you encouraged by what John says to each group?

_____

4. What is the source of our victory over the evil one (vv. 13-14)?

On a daily basis, how can that truth help us overcome his tactics and schemes?

_____

5. Compare John's warning against worldliness (vv. 15-17) with what he says about the world elsewhere (2:2; 3:13; 4:4-5; 5:4-5, 19). What is the meaning of the word _world_ here?

_____

6. Why can there be no middle ground between our love for God and love for the world (vv. 15-17)?

7. How would you explain each of the three worldly desires John mentions in verse 16?

In what ways do these desires manifest themselves today?

8. What are the reasons why we are to resist such temptations (vv. 15-17)?

9. How does the realization that the world is passing away (v. 17) lessen its appeal in your life?

10. How does this passage help us gain a better understanding of our spiritual battle?

4
How Important Is Theology?
1 John 2:18-27

T here is an increasingly popular mindset within the church today which seeks to divorce Christian teaching from Christian living. "We don't want more theology," we are told, "just more about Jesus." But how can we learn more about Jesus apart from a proper understanding of who he is and what he has accomplished? The fact is, there is nothing more basic to Christianity than the person and work of Christ. Apart from understanding Christ, there can be no real Christian living. That is why John goes to great lengths to protect his "dear children" from false views about Christ and to instruct them in the truth. Right thinking leads to right living.

1. What false views about Jesus Christ are popular today?

2. Read 1 John 2:18-27. What characteristics of false teachers and their teaching is John exposing in these verses?

3. All the New Testament authors viewed the first coming of Christ as the event which marked the beginning of the end—"the last hour." What are some of the signs of the last hour (vv. 18-19)?

4. What does John tell us about the relationship between our presence in the church and our perseverance in the faith (v. 19)?

5. Truth is the most effective defense against an onslaught of error. What is the "anointing" that gives us such knowledge of the truth (vv. 20-21; also v. 27)?

6. To deny that "Jesus is the Christ" (v. 22) is to deny that the man Jesus is the eternal, divine Christ—the God-Man. Why is John so harsh toward those who believe and teach such a view (vv. 22-23)?

7. Why is remaining in the truth so important in the Christian life (vv. 24-25)?

8. How do verses 18-27 serve to fulfill John's purpose for writing this portion of his letter (v. 26)?

9. What can we learn from his approach that will help us not to be led astray by false teaching?

10. Obviously John is not suggesting that all human teachers are unnecessary (v. 27), or else he would not have written this epistle. In light of the problem he is addressing, what then is he saying?

11. How does his instruction (v. 27) help us understand what it means to remain in Christ?

12. What does this passage teach us about the Holy Spirit's ministry of *preserving* us from error?

What does it teach about our responsibility of *persevering* in the truth?

5
Like Father, Like Son

1 John 2:28—3:10

A number of years ago *Newsweek Magazine* featured an article on the increasing amount of people within our society who are claiming to be "born again." The article included the following report:

> According to a recent Gallop survey based on personal interviews with 1,553 Americans of voting age, half of all Protestants—and a third of all Americans—say they have been 'born again.' That figure comes to nearly 50 million adult Americans who claim to have experienced a turning point in their lives by making a personal commitment to Jesus Christ as their Savior.[1]

How would we go about discovering if the results of that survey were true? Where would we turn in God's Word to validate such a claim? Without question, 1 John 2:28—3:10 provides one of the clearest tests in Scripture for determining whether one who claims to be a Christian has truly been born of God.

---

1. What do you think your local community would be like if one-third of everyone who lived there was born again?

---

2. Read 1 John 2:28—3:10. Based on John's emphasis at the beginning and the end of the passage (2:28-29; 3:9-10), what test is he using to validate a person's claim of being born again?

3. Why is our continuance in Christ the basis of our confidence at his coming (v. 28)?

4. Throughout this passage John teaches that God's children resemble their Father. In what ways does he reinforce this principle (2:29—3:10)?

5. J. I. Packer writes: "The New Testament gives us two yardsticks of measuring God's love. The first is the cross (see Rom 5:8; 1 Jn 4:8-10); the second is the gift of sonship."[2] How does the realization that we are God's children help us grasp the greatness of his love for us (3:1)?

6. How does the hope (confident assurance) of Christ's appearing (vv. 2-3) serve as a purifying influence in your life?

7. How does John's definition of sin (v. 4) compare with some of the viewpoints people have today?

8. Although Christians can and do sin, how does knowing Christ change our relationship to sin (v. 6)?

What do you think John means by "keeps on sinning" and "continues to sin" (v. 6)?

9. What specifically is the deception John warns against in this passage (v. 7)?

Is this a common error in people's thinking today? Explain.

10. Why does the new birth make it impossible for God's children to have a life characterized by sin (v. 9)?

11. Since the universal fatherhood of God is not taught in Scripture, our spiritual parentage is either from God or the devil. How do we know to which family we belong (v. 10)?

12. As one who has been born of God, what are some ways you see the family traits of obedience and love developing in your life?

[1]"Born Again," *Newsweek Magazine,* October 25, 1976, p. 68.
[2]J. I. Packer, *Knowing God* (Downers Grove, Ill.: InterVarsity Press, 1973), p. 194.

6
Blessed Assurance

1 John 3:11-24

In his classic book *Holiness,* J. C. Ryle expresses concern for believers who doubt: "I heartily wish that assurance was more sought after than it is. Too many among those who believe begin doubting and go on doubting, live doubting and die doubting, and go to heaven in a kind of mist.[1] He goes on to say:

Doubts and fears have power to spoil much of the happiness of a true believer in Christ. Uncertainty and suspense are bad enough in any condition—in the matter of our health, our property, our families, our affections, our earthly callings—but never so bad as in the affairs of our souls.[2]

Without question, doubt and fear have robbed many of the joy of Christian assurance. That is why this passage is so important for Christian living. It overflows with the confidence and assurance that ought to characterize every member of God's family.

---

1. Have you ever questioned whether you were a member of God's family? Explain.

---

2. Read 1 John 3:11-24. John begins this passage by talking about love and hate. How do Cain and Able illustrate the two basic categories of humanity (vv. 11-15)?

3. How do verses 14-15 answer those who claim assurance is based solely on our profession of faith?

4. Why is Christ's death on the cross the supreme example of love (v. 16)?

5. In verse 17 John mentions one specific way we can follow Christ's example. How have you and those in your church sought to love those with material needs?

In what other practical ways might we "lay down our lives" for each other?

6. How can John's assurances in verses 19-20 help us deal with times of doubt?

7. Why would our obedience to God's commands affect our confidence in prayer (vv. 21-22)?

8 Why do you think John reduces the commandments to a single command to be obeyed (v. 23)?

9. Both outwardly and inwardly, how can we know Christ lives in us (v. 24)?

Why are both types of assurance important?

10. Based on this passage, how would you counsel someone who lacked assurance that he or she was a Christian?

¹J. C. Ryle, *Holiness* (Grand Rapids, Mich.: Baker, 1979), p. 158.
²Ryle, *Holiness,* p. 159.

7
Discernment
& Devotion
1 John 4:1-12

Every Christian virtue bears within itself the seeds of its own destruction. A zeal for the truth, for example, if not tempered by love and compassion, can cause us to become arrogant, harsh and cold. Likewise, love for others, if unchecked by the truth, can cause us to be wishy-washy and even tolerant toward sin. If one of these virtues is not governed by the other, it can become a liability and not a strength. Like everything else, obtaining a proper balance is of utmost importance.

In this passage, both doctrinal discernment and devotion to other Christians are held before us in perfect balance. They are not either/or, but both/and. One without the other is not enough.

1. Which of these two aspects of the Christian life do you tend to emphasize above the other? Why?

2. Read 1 John 4:1-12. Why is there such a great need for Christians to be discerning (v. 1)?

What false prophets are active in the world today?

---

3. What test does John give us for determining whether a person's teaching is from "the Spirit of God" or the "spirit of the antichrist" (vv. 2-3)?

Does this mean that everyone who believes in the incarnation of Christ is "from God"? Explain.

---

4. As Christians, how can we overcome the doctrinal errors that continually confront us (v. 4)?

---

5. What additional test does John provide for discerning whether a person's teaching is "from the world" or "from God" (vv. 5-6)?

How does John's test differ from the attitude of doctrinal superiority found in some Christian groups?

---

6. Why must we be diligent in our devotion to one another (vv. 7-8)?

7. What does John mean when he says, "God is love" (v. 8)?

8. How does the cross of Christ demonstrate the manner in which "God so loved us" (vv. 9-11)?

9. How does God's love for you motivate you to love others (v. 11)?

10. How does our love for each other make the invisible God visible in our midst (v. 12)?

11. In what practical way can you show love this week to a brother or sister in Christ?

8
Fear's Remedy
1 John 4:13-21

In the sequel to *Pilgrim's Progress,* Mr. Great-heart and Father Honest engage in a conversation about an old friend, Mr. Fearing. At one point in the dialogue he is portrayed in the following way: "He was a man that had the root of the matter in him, but he was one of the most troublesome Pilgrims that I ever met with in all my days."

That is Bunyan's way of describing many who are on the road to heaven: thoroughly sincere (the root of the matter is in them), yet so overloaded with doubts and fears that their pilgrimage is indeed "troublesome." How is Mr. Fearing to fare in this life? How does he, and how do we, overcome this kind of problem? The answer, in part, lies within this passage in 1 John.

1. Why do you think fear can so easily overcome us?

2. Read 1 John 4:13-21. What three tests does John give for determining whether "we live in him and he in us" (vv. 13-16)?

3. According to John, how is our testimony about Christ related to our experience of God's presence and love (vv. 14-16)?

4. How is our experience of God's love related to our ability to love others (vv. 16, 19)?

5. Why does our love for others enable us to be confident on the day of judgment (vv. 17-18)?

6. What insights does verse 18 give us into why we sometimes fear God and others?

7. How can the principle "perfect love drives out fear" (v. 18) help us overcome our fears?

8. If we have difficulty loving other Christians, what might be the root of the problem (v. 19)?

How does this verse also suggest a solution?

9. Why is it impossible to love God and yet hate one of the members of his family (vv. 20-21)?

10. In what ways can this passage strengthen our confidence before God?

9
Faith Is the Victory

1 John 5:1-12

Christians with a variety of theological views have wholeheartedly sung the words to the well-known hymn:
"Faith is the victory! Faith is the victory!
O glorious victory, That overcomes the world."
But in light of the daily battles in the Christian life, not all agree on what this victory is, when it is accomplished, or how we go about achieving it. In this passage John clears up some of our confusion. He focuses our attention not only on the victory we have in Christ, but also on Christ himself. For, first and foremost, overcoming faith is one that is centered in a correct understanding of who Christ is.

1. What are some of the more popular ways the "victorious Christian life" is being portrayed today?

2. Read 1 John 5:1-12. What are some inevitable results of the new birth (vv. 1-2)?

How are these results related to each other?

3. Why is obedience to God's commandments not burdensome for Christians (v. 3)?

How then can we explain the struggle we sometimes have to obey?

4. Reflect for a moment on the two major characteristics of the world described earlier (see 2:15-17; 4:1-6). What then does it mean for us to "overcome the world" (vv. 4-5)?

When and how does this victory take place (vv. 4-5)?

5. What evidence of this victory do you see in your life?

6. The heretics of John's day taught that the divine Christ descended on Jesus at his baptism but left *before* his death (v. 6). What is wrong with this view?

7. How does the fact that Jesus Christ came by water (symbolizing his baptism) *and* blood (symbolizing his death) refute that heresy (v. 6)?

8. The Old Testament law required two or three witnesses to prove a claim. Who are John's three witnesses, and what do they testify (vv. 7-8)?

9. Why should we accept this threefold testimony concerning God's Son (v. 9)?

10. How does your own experience confirm the truth that eternal life is found in Jesus (vv. 10-12)?

11. Take time to thank God for his Son, and for the victory and eternal life we have in him.

10
What We Know as Christians
1 John 5:13-21

Almost immediately after his well-known conversion experience at Aldersgate Street, John Wesley struggled for months over the uncertainty of his own salvation. Receiving little help from his friends or his church, his thoughts began to turn inward. Focusing on his sinful failures, he became increasingly despondent and dejected. He sought relief by opening passages within the Bible at random, but when that also proved unfruitful he continued his downward spiral. Finally he sank to such depths of despair that he made the following shocking notation in his journal: "My friends affirm that I am mad because I said I was not a Christian a year ago. I affirm I am not a Christian now."[1]

What was Wesley's problem? Unfortunately, it is the same problem that afflicts many sincere Christians today—a lack of knowledge. There are certain truths that all of us as Christians must know if we are to avoid an experience like his. Those truths are found in this passage.

---

1. How well can you relate to Wesley's experience? Explain.

---

2. Read 1 John 5:13-21. What assurances does John give us in these verses?

3. Verse 13 is a summary statement of purpose for the entire epistle. What then are those "things" which assure us we have eternal life?

How would you respond to those who say it is presumptuous to claim we *know* we have eternal life?

4. How can we be assured that our prayers will be answered (vv. 14-15; see also 3:21-22)?

5. How can we get to the point where we want what God wants?

6. Verses 16-17 provide one illustration of the kind of prayer that can be made with confidence. For whom should we be praying? Why?

7. In light of the whole context of this epistle, what might be the distinction between the sin which does not lead to death and the one that does?

8. Why would John not encourage prayer for a person involved in the sin that leads to death?

9. Another New Testament author writes: "Your enemy the devil prowls around like a roaring lion looking for someone to devour" (1 Pet 5:8). In light of this danger, how are you encouraged by John's assurance in verses 18-19?

10. How do we know we belong to God's family and not the world's (v. 19)?

11. How does the coming of God's Son enable us to know the true God in contrast to the false conceptions of God that continually surround us (vv. 20-21)?

12. What certainties in this passage are the most encouraging to you?

---

[1]Arnold A. Dallimore, *George Whitefield,* Vol. I (Carlisle, Penn.: Banner of Truth, 1975), p. 196.

11
Truth
& Love

2 John

There are two equally extreme misconceptions many people have concerning what it means to be a Christian or to live the Christian life. One view says, "It doesn't matter what you believe as long as you are sincere and loving." The other one says, "It doesn't matter how you live as long as you believe the truth." The reason why both views are just as wrong is because the Word of God binds both truth and love inseparably together. They are friends, not enemies. Nowhere will you see this perspective more clearly than in John's second epistle. His major purpose is to demonstrate how love and truth are designed to support and complement one another as only good friends can.

1. Have you ever been in a situation where you felt you were torn between doing the right thing and the loving thing? Explain.

2. Read 2 John. In the brief introductory address and greeting (vv. 1-3), notice how many times *truth* and *love* are mentioned together. What does it mean to love someone "in the truth" (v. 1)?

3. We tend to love only those Christians who agree with us or who we feel are compatible with us. But what does it mean to love them "because of the truth" (v. 2)?

4. In verses 4-6 the unity of truth and love is applied to our relationships within the church. What distinction is made between the *commandment* and the *commandments?*

5. How does our obedience to the *commandments* enable us to fulfill the *commandment*—and vice versa?

6. What specific commands in Scripture have helped you know how to love someone?

7. In verses 7-11 the unity of truth and love is applied to our relationships outside the church. By denying that Christ had come in the flesh (v. 7), what fundamental truths were the false teachers rejecting?

What are some modern counterparts to this kind of heresy?

8. Obtaining a future reward for faithful service was a strong motivation for John (v. 8). In what sense does the prospect of receiving a reward from Jesus

Christ motivate you to walk in truth and love?

9. In view of the fact that these false teachers were traveling about from place to place, what specifically is being prohibited in verses 9-11?

10. What are some other situations in which John's instruction would and would not apply today?

11. Would you identify yourself as someone whose truth needs to be balanced by love or whose love needs to be balanced by truth? Explain.

12. What can you do to gain a better balance?

12
Opening Our Hearts
& Homes

3 John

Imagine living in a world where there were no bed and breakfasts, no hotels and headwaiters. If traveling evangelists and teachers were to come to your town, you would have the privilege of inviting them into your home for the night and giving them provisions for their journey. Such was the world of John and his readers. Their hospitality was one of the clearest testimonies of their love for the brethren and obedience to God.

The same is true today. For in the words of Helga Henry, wife of noted theologian Carl F. H. Henry, "Christian hospitality is not a matter of choice; it is not a matter of money; it is not a matter of age, social standing, sex, or personality. Christian hospitality is a matter of obedience to God."[1] For that reason the instruction concerning hospitality in this letter takes on added significance.

---

1. Have you had much opportunity to be involved in the ministry of hospitality? Explain.

---

2. Read 3 John. Why is Gaius an especially good example for us to follow (vv. 2-4)?

3. What does it mean for us to be "walking in the truth" (vv. 3-4)?

4. How are both love and faithfulness demonstrated in Christian hospitality (vv. 5-6)?

5. What does it mean for us to show hospitality "in a manner worthy of God" (v. 6)?

6. Why do you think Christian workers are to look to Christians for support and not to non-Christians (vv. 7-8)?

7. In addition to hospitality, how else can we "work together" with such people?

8. How are the actions of Diotrephes consistent with his true heart's desire (vv. 9-11)?

9. If we desire to be first, how will that conflict with our ability to be loving?

10. In contrast to Diotrephes, Demetrius was "well spoken of by everyone" (v. 12). If those who know you best were asked about your love and hospitality, what might they say?

11. In light of this passage, what practical steps could you take to develop more of a ministry of hospitality?

---

[1]V. A. Hall, *Be My Guest* (Chicago: Moody Press, 1979), p. 9.

13
John's Letters in Review

W e are no longer confronted with the false teachers of John's day. Yet their modern-day counterparts are just as troublesome for us as they were for his readers. Cult members, for example, regularly knock on our doors, distributing pamphlets and presenting distorted views about Christ. Many "progressive" theologians deny the deity of Christ and urge us to accept a merely human Jesus. Leading authorities on ethics claim that standards of right and wrong are totally subjective and relative. For these and other reasons, it is important to review the applications of John's teachings for today.

1. In 1 John there are no less than six references to the new birth (2:29; 3:9; 4:7; 5:1, 4, 18). According to John, what are some of the inevitable results of that experience?

2. How would you respond to a person who says that he is a Christian regardless of how he lives because he has professed faith in Christ?

3. Why is it impossible to have fellowship with those who have not truly been born of God's Spirit?

What does this say about being involved in today's ecumenical movement or in a church that does not accept the fundamentals of the faith?

4. The moral enticements of the world seem to be getting stronger every day. How do John's letters help us to realize and resist the world's influence?

5. How can John's letters help you to respond to the Mormons or Jehovah's Witnesses next time they knock on your door?

6. Concerning the Christian faith, F. F. Bruce has written, "Continuance is the test of reality."[1] How do John's letters support that statement, especially in view of his emphasis on "remaining" (or abiding) in Christ?

7. Professing Christians who choose to continue in sin are often described as "backsliders" or "carnal Christians" in an attempt to explain their behavior. What perspectives have John's letters given you about such people?

8. How have these letters changed your understanding of the Christian life?

9. How have they changed your understanding of *living* the Christian life?

---

[1]Bruce, *The Epistles of John,* p. 69.

Leader's Notes

Leading a Bible discussion can be an enjoyable and rewarding experience. But it can also be *scary*—especially if you've never done it before. If this is your feeling, you're in good company. When God asked Moses to lead the Israelites out of Egypt, he replied, "O Lord, please send someone else to do it!" (Ex 4:13).

When Solomon became king of Israel, he felt the task was far beyond his abilities. "I am only a little child and do not know how to carry out my duties. . . . Who is able to govern this great people of yours?" (1 Kings 3:7, 9).

When God called Jeremiah to be a prophet, he replied, "Ah, Sovereign LORD, . . . I do not know how to speak; I am only a child" (Jer 1:6).

The list goes on. The apostles were "unschooled, ordinary men" (Acts 4:13). Timothy was young, frail and frightened. Paul's "thorn in the flesh" made him feel weak. But God's response to all of his servants—including you—is essentially the same: "My grace is sufficient for you" (2 Cor 12:9). Relax. God helped these people in spite of their weaknesses, and he can help you in spite of your feelings of inadequacy.

There is another reason why you should feel encouraged. Leading a Bible discussion is not difficult if you follow certain guidelines. You don't need to be an expert on the Bible or a trained teacher. The suggestions listed below should enable you to effectively and enjoyably fulfill your role as leader.

Preparing to Lead

1. Ask God to help you understand and apply the passage to your own life. Unless this happens, you will not be prepared to lead others. Pray too for the various members of the group. Ask God to give you an enjoyable and profitable time together studying his Word.

2. As you begin each study, read and reread the assigned Bible passage to familiarize yourself with what the author is saying. In the case of book studies, you may want to read through the entire book prior to the first study. This will give you a helpful overview of its contents.

3. This study guide is based on the New International Version of the Bible. It will help you and the group if you use this translation as the basis for your study and discussion. Encourage others to use the NIV also, but allow them the freedom to use whatever translation they prefer.

4. Carefully work through each question in the study. Spend time in meditation and reflection as you formulate your answers.

5. Write your answers in the space provided in the study guide. This will help you to express your understanding of the passage clearly.

6. It might help you to have a Bible dictionary handy. Use it to look up any unfamiliar words, names or places. (For additional help on how to study a passage, see chapter five of *Leading Bible Discussions,* IVP.)

7. Once you have finished your own study of the passage, familiarize yourself with the leader's notes for the study you are leading. These are designed to help you in several ways. First, they tell you the purpose the study guide author had in mind while writing the study. Take time to think through how the study questions work together to accomplish that purpose. Second, the notes provide you with additional background information or comments on some of the questions. This information can be useful if people have difficulty understanding or answering a question. Third, the leader's notes can alert you to potential problems you may encounter during the study.

8. If you wish to remind yourself of anything mentioned in the leader's notes, make a note to yourself below that question in the study.

Leading the Study

1. Begin the study on time. Unless you are leading an evangelistic Bible study, open with prayer, asking God to help you to understand and apply the passage.

2. Be sure that everyone in your group has a study guide. Encourage them to prepare beforehand for each discussion by working through the questions in the guide.

3. At the beginning of your first time together, explain that these studies are meant to be discussions not lectures. Encourage the members of the group to participate. However, do not put pressure on those who may be hesitant to speak during the first few sessions.

4. Read the introductory paragraph at the beginning of the discussion. This will orient the group to the passage being studied.

5. Read the passage aloud if you are studying one chapter or less. You may choose to do this yourself, or someone else may read if he or she has been asked to do so prior to the study. Longer passages may occasionally be read in parts at different times during the study. Some studies may cover several chapters. In such cases reading aloud would probably take too much time, so the group members should simply read the assigned passages prior to the study.

6. As you begin to ask the questions in the guide, keep several things in mind. First, the questions are designed to be used just as they are written. If you wish, you may simply read them aloud to the group. Or you may prefer to express them in your own words. However, unnecessary rewording of the questions is not recommended.

Second, the questions are intended to guide the group toward understanding and applying the *main idea* of the passage. The author of the guide has stated his or her view of this central idea in the *purpose* of the study in the leader's notes. You should try to understand how the passage expresses this idea and how the study questions work together to lead the group in that direction.

There may be times when it is appropriate to deviate from the study guide. For example, a question may have already been answered. If so, move on to the next question. Or someone may raise an important question not covered in the guide. Take time to discuss it! The important thing is to use discretion. There may be many routes you can travel to reach the goal of the study. But the easiest route is usually the one the author has suggested.

7. Avoid answering your own questions. If necessary, repeat or rephrase them until they are clearly understood. An eager group quickly becomes passive and silent if they think the leader will do most of the talking.

8. Don't be afraid of silence. People may need time to think about the question before formulating their answers.

9. Don't be content with just one answer. Ask, "What do the rest of you think?" or "Anything else?" until several people have given answers to the question.

10. Acknowledge all contributions. Try to be affirming whenever possible. Never reject an answer. If it is clearly wrong, ask, "Which verse led you to that conclusion?" or again, "What do the rest of you think?"

11. Don't expect every answer to be addressed to you, even though this will probably happen at first. As group members become more at ease, they will begin to truly interact with each other. This is one sign of a healthy discussion.

12. Don't be afraid of controversy. It can be very stimulating. If you don't resolve an issue completely, don't be frustrated. Move on and keep it in mind for later. A subsequent study may solve the problem.

13. Stick to the passage under consideration. It should be the source for answering the questions. Discourage the group from unnecessary cross-referencing. Likewise, stick to the subject and avoid going off on tangents.

14. Periodically summarize what the *group* has said about the passage. This helps to draw together the various ideas mentioned and gives continuity to the study. But don't preach.

15. Conclude your time together with conversational prayer. Be sure to ask God's help to apply those things which you learned in the study.

16. End on time.

Many more suggestions and helps are found in *Leading Bible Discussions* (IVP). Reading and studying through that would be well worth your time.

Components of Small Groups

A healthy small group should do more than study the Bible. There are four components you should consider as you structure your time together.

Nurture. Being a part of a small group should be a nurturing and edifying experience. You should grow in your knowledge and love of God and each other. If we are to properly love God, we must know and keep his commandments (Jn 14:15). That is why Bible study should be a foundational part of your small group. But you can be nurtured by other things as well. You can memorize Scripture, read and discuss a book, or occasionally listen to a tape of a good speaker.

Community. Most people have a need for close friendships. Your small group can be an excellent place to cultivate such relationships. Allow time for informal interaction before and after the study. Have a time of sharing during the meeting. Do fun things together as a group, such as a potluck supper or a picnic. Have someone bring refreshments to the meeting. Be creative!

Worship. A portion of your time together can be spent in worship and prayer. Praise God together for who he is. Thank him for what he has done and is doing in your lives and in the world. Pray for each other's needs. Ask God to help you to apply what you have learned. Sing hymns together.

Mission. Many small groups decide to work together in some form of outreach. This can be a practical way of applying what you have learned. You can host a series of evangelistic discussions for your friends or neighbors. You can visit people at a home for the elderly. Help a widow with cleaning or repair jobs around her home. Such projects can have a transforming influence on your group.

For a detailed discussion of the nature and function of small groups, read *Small Group Leaders' Handbook* or *Good Things Come in Small Groups* (both from IVP).

Study 1. Fellowship & Forgiveness. 1 John 1:1-10.

Purpose: To understand the basis for having true fellowship with other Christians and with God.

Question 2. This initial emphasis on the incarnation of Christ is due to the fact that John's readers were being confronted with an early form of heresy known as Gnosticism (see the introduction to the guide). Its central teaching was that the spirit is entirely good and matter is entirely evil. This type of dualism also resulted in a denial of Christ's true humanity. This particular false teaching provides the backdrop for a good deal within John's letter (see 2:22, 23; 4:2, 3; 5:6-8).

Question 5. Gnosticism also taught that the question of obedience to God's commandments had no bearing on an individual's relationship to God. Viewed against such a background, this entire section is designed to expose those who were making such claims for what they truly were—unbelieving heretics (vv. 6, 8, 10), At the same time, it is also designed to assure John's readers of the basis of true fellowship with a holy and righteous God (vv. 7, 9).

Question 7. It is important to remember that two lifestyles are being contrasted in these verses: one is characterized by error and sin; the other by truth and righteousness. In view of the other similar contrasts that will emerge in this letter (2:3-6; 3:6-9) and the terms that are used in this passage to describe those who do not enjoy fellowship with God (vv. 6, 8, 10), it seems clear that John's contrast is between true Christians and those who merely profess to be Christians.

Question 8. Verse 9 is often used to teach that our moment-by-moment fellowship with God is dependent on confessing our sins. According to this view, Christians who deny their sins are out of fellowship with God, while those who confess their sins remain in fellowship with him.

But in view of the apparent contrast between Christians and non-Christians within the preceding verses (vv. 6-7), it is more likely that John has the same contrast in mind in verses 8-10. Just as our moral lifestyle determines the reality of our claim to have fellowship with God, so also does our attitude toward sin. If we confess the guilt of our sin, John assures us that we have entered into a saving fellowship with God (v. 9). But if we deny we are guilty of sin, John concludes that we have no saving fellowship with God at all (vv. 8, 10)

Study 2. Talking & Walking the Truth. 1 John 2:1-11.

Purpose: To realize that we must look beyond what we say to what we do in order to be certain about the reality of our faith.

Question 2. John often speaks in such absolute contrasts that he seems to deny that Christians sin. This verse is especially important, therefore, in giving us a balanced view of John's teaching.

Question 3. The word translated as "atoning sacrifice" (v. 2) is borrowed from the Old Testament sacrificial system. The wrath of God was turned away from the sinner who offered an acceptable animal sacrifice. As our true sacrifice, Jesus Christ turned away God's wrath from us by dying on the cross. Because of his death, Jesus does not literally need to speak to God in our defense—his death speaks loudly and clearly.

Question 4. Be sure to keep in mind that what is being described within these verses is our general lifestyle, not an occasional breaking of God's commands. Certainly Christians can and do sin, as John indicates in verses 1-2.

God's love (v. 5) can have one of two meanings: (a) God's love for us, which is made complete when it moves us to obedience; (b) our love for God, which is made complete when it is demonstrated by obedience.

Question 6. Although the biblical command to love is old, Jesus Christ has invested it with a richer and deeper meaning. The old command was "love your neighbor as yourself" (Lev 19:18). The new command is: "Love one another. As I have loved you, so you must love one another" (Jn 13:34). This command is new for two reasons. First, it is new in its object: "love one another—that is, other Christians. Second, it is new in its standard: "as I have loved you." Christ's death on the cross becomes the new measure of our love. As John says later in his letter, "This is how we know what love is: Jesus Christ laid down his life for us. And we ought to lay down our lives for our brothers" (1 Jn 3:16).

Study 3. Encouragement & Warning. 1 John 2:12-17.

Purpose: To encourage us in view of our spiritual attainments and to warn us in view of our spiritual enemies.

Question 2. It may be helpful to review with the group the somewhat severe statements that John has just made concerning obedience (2:3-6) and love (2:7-11): "He does not mean to give his readers the impression that he thinks they are in darkness or that he doubts the reality of their faith. It is the false teachers whom he regards as spurious, not the loyal members of the church. So he digresses to tell them his view of their Christian standing" (Stott, *The Epistles of John,* p. 95).

Question 3. There have been various suggestions concerning how to interpret these figurative expressions. Probably the best approach is to understand the reference to the "little children" as one which embraces all the readers (see 2:1); the "fathers" as representing those who are older in the faith; the "young men" as those who are younger in the faith.

Question 4. As Jesus did in the wilderness, we need to use specific scriptural truths in order to overcome the specific schemes and falsehoods of the evil one (see Mt 4:4, 7, 10). The Christian who does not understand God's Word adequately cannot use it adequately. See also Revelation 12:10-11.

Question 5. Remember that the term *world* has numerous meanings in the New Testament, depending on the context in which it is found. Here John is emphasizing the way in which the world system thinks and acts apart from God, as this context clearly indicates.

Study 4. How Important Is Theology? 1 John 2:18-27.

Purpose: To confirm that the teaching ministry of the Holy Spirit is our defense against those who would have us believe that Jesus is not the Christ.

Question 2. The meaning of the word *antichrist* is important to understand. It is formed by joining two words together: *Christ* and the prefix *anti,* which in this context means "against." As "antichrists," their false teaching concentrates on opposing and denying the truth that the man Jesus is the divine, eternal Christ (v. 22). They are identified "not as those who are outside the Church, but as those who at least for a time were within it. In other words, they are not the outright pagan opponents of Christianity but rather those who were attempting to destroy the faith from within by pretending to be Christians" (James M. Boice, *The Epistles of John* [Grand Rapids, Mich.: Zondervan, 1983], pp. 85-86)

Question 4. Since those who are born of God are characterized by overcoming faith (1 Jn 5:4), they cannot apostatize, or depart from the faith. While apostasy is possible for those who have merely professed saving faith in Christ, it is not possible for genuine believers. Saving faith enables us to continue in our faith and in our identity with others of like faith.

Question 5. The indwelling presence of the Holy Spirit is the fundamental means of understanding the truth of God's Word and of using what we learn to combat heresy. Specifically, John is referring to the Spirit's ministry of illumination, or the revealing of God's truth to our hearts (see 1 Cor 2:12, 15-16).

Question 7. The second way that we combat doctrinal error is by holding fast to the basic truths of the gospel which we have heard from the beginning, as opposed to neglecting them in search of some new teaching. As Paul told Timothy: "But as for you, continue in what you have learned and have become convinced of" (2 Tim 3:14) It is this continuance in the truths of God's Word that assures us of God's promise to us: eternal life.

Question 11. In light of the context, both here and throughout the letter, abiding in Christ is continuing, or remaining, in the truths about Christ. It is, therefore, the mark of *all* genuine believers, not just a select few. Remaining in Christ means persevering in the faith.

Study 5. Like Father, Like Son. 1 John 2:28—3:10.

Purpose: To demonstrate that those who are born of a righteous God will live a righteous life.

Question 2. In these verses we now have the second cycle of tests beginning to unfold. Here the test is the same one that was first introduced in 1:5-10 and then in 2:3-6. It is the moral test, or the test of obedience to Christ's commands.

Question 4. In verse 29 we are introduced to the concept of having been "born of God." Previously John has described believers as those who "know" God (2:3-4, 13-14), are "in him" (2:5-6) and "in the light" (2:9-10), and who "remain" in the Father and in the Son (2:24, 27-28). But John emphasizes that this birth from above imparts the life of God within us and is responsible for our family likeness (see also 3:9; 4:7-8; 5:1, 4, 18).

Question 7. The point of this question is to underscore how so many today underestimate the seriousness of sin. It is not merely "missing the mark" of God's righteousness, nor of departing from what is right; it is an active rebellion against God's revealed will and a deliberate violation of his holy law. Acknowledging this is absolutely fundamental to living a holy life: "He that wishes to attain right views about Christian holiness, must begin by examining the vast and solemn subject of sin" (J. C. Ryle, *Holiness* [Grand Rapids, Mich.: Baker, 1979], p. 1).

Question 9. The moral deception that is in view here is just as dangerous as the doctrinal deception that was addressed in the previous passage (see 2:26). It comes under the broad banner of "antinomianism," which says that because we are under the grace of God, we no longer are bound to any moral law. In other words, these false teachers were emphasizing that it is possible to *be* righteous without ever attempting to *practice* righteousness.

Question 10. One of the best explanations of this difficult verse comes from John Stott: "The new birth involves the acquisition of a new nature through the implanting within us of the very seed or lifegiving power of God. Birth from God is a deep, radical, inward transformation. Moreover, the new nature received at the new birth remains. It exerts a strong internal pressure towards holiness. It is the abiding influence of His seed within everyone who is born of God, which enables John to affirm without fear of contradiction that he cannot go on living in sin" (Stott, *The Epistles of John,* p. 127).

Study 6. Blessed Assurance. 1 John 3:11-24.

Purpose: To show that the evidence of a right standing before God is a sacrificial love for other Christians.

Question 2. With these verses we are again introduced to the social test, or the test of love (see 2:7-11). Do not fail to note that in each of these tests John takes us back to the basic truth that has been heard "from the beginning" (v. 11; see also 1:5; 2:24). Whether it concerns our conduct or our convictions about Christ, John's appeal rests on the unchanging foundational truths of the gospel.

Question 3. Assurance of salvation comes through a threefold witness: (a) the testimony of God's Word (1 Jn 5:10-12); (b) the testimony of the Holy Spirit (1 Jn 3:24); and (c) the testimony of a changed life, which is John's overwhelming emphasis in this letter. 1 John 3:14-15 is but one application of this latter testimony.

Question 6. It is important to realize that the beginning phrase of verse 19, "this then is how we know," points back to what has just been stated in verses 16-18. The next verse (20) then goes on to give us an additional reason for our assurance.

Question 9. "But if we intend to obey His commandments, let us see what He commands. He does not separate faith from love, but demands of us that both . . . mutually embrace one another. This is why he puts the word *commandment* in the singular. But this is a remarkable passage, for he defines clearly and briefly what the complete perfection of a holy life consists in" (John Calvin, *The First Epistle of John* [Grand Rapids, Mich.: Baker Books, 1979], p. 281).

Study 7. Discernment & Devotion. 1 John 4:1-12.

Purpose: To demonstrate that the indwelling presence of God's Spirit enables us to confess Jesus as Christ and to love one another.

Question 2. In giving us a further explanation of the doctrinal test, John begins by again reminding us that not every "spirit" is to be believed. The word *spirit* means either an utterance or a person "inspired by a spirit," and points us to the fact that a person's teaching is inspired either by God or Satan. The danger of demonic deception cannot be underestimated within the church today.

Question 3. Modern-day representatives of "the spirit of antichrist" include members of the major cults and liberal theologians and their followers who deny the incarnation of Christ.

Question 7. This description of God does not reduce him to an abstract quality, but primarily refers to his action: "Its effect is to claim that *all* God's action is loving. Since love is a personal activity, the statement stresses the personality of God to the fullest extent. At the same time, the immense gulf between God and men is expressed; of no man could it possibly be said that he *is* love. Only God is completely loving" (I. Howard Marshall, *The Epistles of John* [Grand Rapids, Mich.: Eerdmans, 1978], p. 213).

Question 10. According to 3:16-18, genuine love will express itself in practical deeds of love. This is the "completed" love of verse 12. John's point is simply this: whenever we actively demonstrate love to other believers, God is seen in our lives because he is the source of our love. In this sense, then, the God whom "no one has ever seen" is seen in our midst. His love is completed because its goal is realized, enabling us to love others.

Study 8. Fear's Remedy. 1 John 4:13-21.

Purpose: To demonstrate that God's love for us enables us to stand confidently before him without fear.

Question 2. These three grounds for assurance could be termed the *internal* witness (v. 13; the presence of the Holy Spirit); the *external* witness (vv. 14-15; the confession that Jesus is the Christ); the *evidential* witness (v. 16; the fruits of the Christian life; in this case, love for one another). All three are essential for Christian assurance.

Question 3. It is simply not enough to affirm the truth that Jesus is God. Our creed must be backed by our conduct, which in turn is the result of knowing and experiencing God's love.

Question 5. If we are Christlike in our love for one another, this is confirming evidence that God, who is love, lives in us. For that reason genuine love is grounds for assurance on the day of judgment.

Question 8. One of the best ways to gain a deeper appreciation of God's love for us is to meditate on what John has already told us; God's love is the reason for our redemption (1 John 4:8-10) and our adoption into his family (1 Jn 3:1). In light of such love for us, how is it possible for us not to love others?

Study 9. Faith Is the Victory. 1 John 5:1-12.

Purpose: To demonstrate that faith in the incarnate Son of God is the means of overcoming the errors and falsehoods of the world system.

Question 3. The point of verses 3-4 is not that the commandments themselves are easy to obey; rather they become easy to obey because of the enabling presence of the indwelling Spirit, brought about through the new birth. The reason for the struggle, then, is due to the ongoing, internal conflict between flesh and spirit.

Question 4. Doctrinally, we triumph over the world's opposition to God's truth (4:1-6) by believing in Jesus as the incarnate Son of God. Morally, too, we triumph over the world's selfish, unloving lifestyle (2:15-17) by faith in Christ, the fruit of which is love for the brethren. This twofold victory over the world is initiated by the new birth and is the progressive experience of everyone born of God.

Question 6. With this emphasis, these false teachers maintained that Jesus was born and died only as a man. Hence, they denied both the incarnation and crucifixion of Jesus as the God-man. Such a denial strikes at the very heart of the gospel message, since only the God-man can atone for our sin and at the same time satisfy God's wrath against sin (2:2; 4:10).

Question 7. The baptism of Jesus testifies to the reality of the incarnation because at that time the Holy Spirit declared: "This is My Son, whom I love; with him I am well pleased" (Mt 3:17). John's primary point is that this same Son of God who was baptized in the Jordan was also the One who died on the cross. This is the One whom believers acknowledge to be the Son of God (v. 5).

Question 8. In addition to the water and blood, the Holy Spirit also testifies that Jesus is the Son of God. The Spirit did this when he descended on Jesus at his baptism (see Jn 1:32-34) and continues to do this through the ministry of God's Word (see Jn 15:26).

Question 10. In contrast to the previous three witnesses, this fourth witness is experienced only by believers. "When a person places his faith in the incarnate Christ, he experiences eternal life with all that such an experience involves (God's Spirit bearing witness with his spirit)" (Donald Burdick, *The Epistles of John* [Chicago: Moody Press, 1970], p. 381).

Study 10. What We Know as Christians. 1 John 5:13-21.

Purpose: To teach us that God has not only given us assurances of knowing him but of receiving answers from him in prayer.

Question 3. It would be helpful at this point to highlight the three tests that John has been weaving throughout this letter. For example, assurance can be tested by obedience to Christ's commandments (2:3-6); love for the brethren (3:11-15); and belief that Jesus is the incarnate Son of God (4:1-6).

Question 4. These two passages represent two of the major conditions for answered prayer in the New Testament and, therefore, ought to be emphasized. Compare also John 15:7.

Questions 7-8. Verses 16-17 are two of the most difficult verses in all of the New Testament. The interpretive issues are complex, but basically there are two broad viewpoints concerning the meaning of "a sin that leads to death":

(1) Believers who continue to live in sin experience the divine discipline of physical death. If we were to pray for their spiritual restoration, then, we should not be surprised if our prayers were not answered. Our request would not be according to God's will. Certainly other passages teach that such divine discipline does occur (see 1 Cor 11:30), but the difficulty here is that John has repeatedly emphasized that genuine believers cannot continue in sin (see 3:9). In fact, he says this very same thing in the next verse (18). Therefore, this is probably not the best interpretation.

(2) Nonbelievers who are characterized by the adamant denial of the truth and willful immorality that John has been exposing throughout this letter will certainly experience spiritual death. If we were to pray for their salvation, then, we should not be surprised that our request was not answered because it would not be according to God's will. Such a persistent denial of Christ by those who were once professing members of the church (see 2:19) is nothing short of apostasy and, therefore, places them beyond the saving grace of God (see Heb 6:4-6). This seems to be the best understanding in light of the context of the letter.

With either view, however, the point of the passage is the same: there are certain requests that will not be answered the way we would like simply because they are not in accordance with God's will. Therefore, the assurance of verses 14-15 is qualified.

Question 10. There are three great words of certainty that are emphasized in this letter: we *are* children of God (3:1); he who has the Son *has* eternal life (5:12); we *know* him who is true (5:19). How fitting, then, for this letter to end in verses 18-20 on such a repeated emphasis of assurance.

Study 11. Truth & Love. 2 John.

Purpose: To demonstrate how our love for others is to be guided and governed by the truth.

Question 2. As the remainder of this letter will reveal, these readers had been exercising love at the expense of truth. In particular, they had been indiscriminately practicing hospitality to all traveling teachers, including those who were rejecting fundamental doctrines of the faith. To love "in the truth," therefore, is to demonstrate a love that is consistent with the truth; it is a love that is governed and guided by the truth.

Question 4. The "commandments" are all of the specific requirements which explain how we are to go about fulfilling the "command" to love one another. A helpful explanation of these verses can be found in Romans 13:8-10.

Question 7. These are the very same false teachers who formed the background to much of what John wrote in his first letter (see 1 Jn 2:18-19; 4:2-3) They are "antichrists" in the sense that they deny Christ's incarnation and thus his deity. Here they are further described as those who "run ahead" of the elementary truths of the gospel. Some of their modern-day counterparts are identified in study 7, question 3, of the leader's notes.

Question 9. Hospitality is the issue that John is addressing. Such instruction, therefore, would not prohibit us from greeting or even conversing with those who come to us with this teaching. What it does prohibit is providing them with any support for their work, such as housing and food. Such a prohibition, then, is a practical application of love that is guided and governed by the truth.

Study 12. Opening Our Hearts & Homes. 3 John.

Purpose: To demonstrate how our commitment to the truth is to be manifested by our love for others.

Question 2. "Walking" in the truth is far different than merely talking about the truth. It is one thing to know the Christian jargon; it is another to live the Christian life. Gaius, therefore, is an excellent illustration of the importance of our "walk matching our talk." See especially 1 John 2:3-6; 4:20-21.

Question 4. Because hospitality is a frequently repeated commandment elsewhere (Rom 12:13; 1 Pet 4:9; Heb 13:2) as well as in this passage (v. 8), it is a very practical demonstration of our faithfulness to God's Word. It is also a very tangible expression of our love for God's people (see 1 Jn 3:16-18).

Question 5. This is the kind of treatment toward others that pleases God and brings praise to his name (see Col 1:10; 1 Thess 2:12). In practical terms, this means that our hospitality is to be done willingly, generously and, above all else, lovingly, not begrudgingly (see 1 Pet 4:9).

Question 8. What is most significant to note about Diotrephes is that he is not one of the false teachers John has been denouncing in these letters. There is no suggestion that he has disagreed with John on any basic point of doctrine. His root problem is personal ambition, which has led him to resist apostolic authority. Everything else in these verses is merely the result of this problem.

Question 10. Demetrius serves as an illustration of the exhortation in verse 11b: "Imitate what is good." In contrast, Diotrephes is the embodiment of what John has in view in verse 11a: "Do not imitate what is evil."

Study 13. John's Letters in Review.

Purpose: To review some of the applications of John's teaching for us today.

Question 1. A twofold emphasis is placed on the new birth in these passages: (1) Certain things are inevitably true of everyone who has been born of God (3:9; 5:4; 18); (2) everyone who has certain fruits in his or her life is identified as being born of God (2:29; 4:7; 5:1). Both perspectives demonstrate the necessary cause-effect relationship between the new birth and the fruits of that birth.

Question 3. The root meaning of the term *fellowship* is a "sharing" in that which is common. Our common faith, based on a common commitment to the truths of the gospel, makes our fellowship with one another possible. See especially 1 John 1:3-4 in light of 2:18-19.

Question 6. The most explicit teaching within these letters in support of such a statement is found in 1 John 2:19. Of the false teachers, John says: "If they had belonged to us, they would have *remained* with us" (my emphasis). This same emphasis on "remaining" or "abiding" in the truth appears over twenty other times within these letters (1 Jn 2:6, 10, 14, 17, 24, 27, 28; 3:6, 9, 14, 15, 17, 24; 4:12, 13, 15, 16; 2 Jn 2, 9).

Question 7. Certainly Christians can and do fall into sin. What John has been stating, however, is that they cannot continue in such sin. The assurance that we have been born of God's Spirit rests on our obedience to Christ's commands, love for the brethren and continued belief in the truth about God's Son. Saving faith, therefore, is a persevering faith—one which continues in holiness and faith.

Ron Blankley is a full-time teaching elder at Emmanuel Bible Church in Schooley's Mountain, New Jersey.